Our prayer is that you
continue to g...
knowledge...

With Love,
Mrs. Berends
Mrs. Vanden Bosch

Amber Sweet

Where Do I Fit In?

Prayers for Young Teen Girls *Young Teens*

Where Do I Fit In?

Dyan LeVander

AUGSBURG Publishing House • Minneapolis

*With gratitude to the teens
of my 1988 Catechism Class,
Megan, Kathy, Lisa, Amy, Heather,
Todd, Ron, Rob, David, Kevin and Scott,
and to my niece, Laura.*

WHERE DO I FIT IN?
Prayers for Young Teen Girls

Copyright © 1989 Augsburg Publishing House

All rights reserved. Except for brief quotations in critical articles or reviews, no part of this book may be reproduced in any manner without prior written permission from the publisher. Write to: Permissions, Augsburg Publishing House, 426 S. Fifth St., Box 1209, Minneapolis MN 55440.

Photos: Paul Buddle, 22, 56; Dave Anderson, 38, 72, 78; CLEO Photography, 94.

Library of Congress Cataloging-in-Publication Data

LeVander, Dyan.
  Where do I fit in?

  1. Teenage girls—Prayer-books and devotions
—English. I. Title.
BV4860.L48   1989   242'.833   89-205
ISBN 0-8066-2398-5

Manufactured in the U.S.A.   APH 10-7094

1 2 3 4 5 6 7 8 9 0 1 2 3 4 5 6 7 8 9

Contents

About This Book   9

Where do I fit in?   11

Just how does it work?   12

Make them stop   13

Do you ever need me, Lord?   14

Counting rainbows   15

Girlfriends with boyfriends   16

For people with AIDS   17

What will you do about the animals?   19

Fresh snow in the morning   21

I don't mean to be rude   23

Am I an awful person?   24

It's too much!   25

Today I won't ask for anything   27

I got an "A"!   28

The man on the steps   29

I hate smoke   31

An old friend's voice   32

Dancing for peace   33

A walk in the woods   34
It's embarrassing to ask questions   35
What is it about boys?   37
Never content   39
Helpless   40
Baby-sitting   41
I made the team   42
A guest in my own homes   43
Waiting for the school bus   44
I can't help it   45
Two sides of me   46
Timeless   48
Please talk to my parents   49
I can't keep up   50
Letting things slide   51
A candle flame   52
Broken promises   53
Dad's out of work   54
I want a date   55
When I'm a woman   57
I'll do it later   58
Mom's getting married   59
Honesty   60
Love is a big feeling   61
Were parents ever teenagers?   62

I'm no quitter 63
Life was so easy 64
When to stop? 66
Faith like his 67
Do something for Sarah 69
My friend doesn't believe 71
What do you look like? 73
Why me? 74
My Asian friend 75
Being shy 76
How can you top this? 77
What's wrong with people? 79
The train 81
Not eating enough 83
An accident 85
Telling secrets 87
Sunday 89
At odds 91
When I get married 93
My rock 95
Being sick is boring 96
Not even once 97
I don't get it! 98
Forgive and forget 99
Looks aren't everything 100

Get well   101
Cold war   103
My mean side   104
Shower solo   105
What to be?   106
Getting a job   107
Bare branches   108
Why won't they come?   110
Adopted   111
Walking on the beach   112

About This Book

Prayers come in all shapes and sizes. They can be long and formal, with fancy words. Or they can be brief and informal, in our own words. Prayers might ask God to help us with our hurts and doubts, or they might not ask for anything at all. Sometimes you want to say thank you when something wonderful happens to you. Usually we talk to God about our *own* problems, and that is good. But I hope this book will encourage you to pray for others: friends and family, people who bother you, and people you've never met who are suffering. God wants to be in touch with you any time, any place; morning, lunchtime, after school, on long, quiet walks by the beach, and when you are tempted to break the rules—God will be waiting, ready to listen.

When we pray, it reminds us that we don't have to carry our load alone. We can share it with God, who understands and accepts us no matter what we do or say. How do we know that?

It's true, we can't *see* God, and some of the prayers in this book admit that frustration. But prayer is trusting in a power bigger than we are. It is an act of faith. And so, it isn't always easy or natural. But the Spirit helps us to try.

My hope is that this book will help you express your feelings to God. Use the names of your own loved ones instead of the ones I used when you read them. And then, be open to being changed by your own prayers, open to letting God help you make important decisions, open to a closer relationship with Jesus. To grow in our prayer life takes time and practice. Be patient. And one more thing. Prayer is a *two-way* street. God needs a chance to speak, too. Don't forget to listen.

Where do I fit in?

God, you thought of a lot of things,
like matching squirrels to the
gray bark of trees.
Lime-green caterpillars and frogs blend
into the grass where they live,
and polar bears come in white
to live safely in their wintry climate.
I want to know where I belong,
where do I fit in?
I'm too old to bother with my little sister,
and too young to go along with my older brother.
I'm too shy to talk to boys
and too clumsy to be a cheerleader.
The chorus is for those who can carry a tune,
and the stage for an actress.
So, tell me, Lord, where do *I* fit in?
Details,
you remembered so many little details
when you made the world.
Tell me, what did you have in mind for me?

▶ Just how does it work?

Sometimes I wonder, God,
who am I talking to?
Am I kidding myself,
praying to the clear, blue sky
that goes on forever—
so high and mysterious
it stretches overhead.
Is there more than that,
I mean, can you really recognize *my* voice?
How is it you *hear* me, God,
with a million ears, or radar, or do you
tape messages and return calls later?
I want to know, just how does it work,
that you hear people's prayers?
They have so far to go to reach you—
wherever you are—don't they?
Some days I think prayer is a crazy idea,
I'm just talking to the breeze,
but I do keep calling to you, Lord,
even with all my questions.
I do keep praying,
when I'm lonely or sad or hurting.
And it helps to share it all with you—
the breezes and the sky couldn't do that,
I know—you *do* hear!
But sometimes I wonder, God,
how?

▶ Make them stop

O God, why do the boys in my class have to be so mean?
What ever did I do to them,
to make them call me ugly names and laugh?
Such cruel words, Lord.
They haunt me and hunt me down in the cafeteria and in the hallways.
They'll find me after school when I leave the building and when I return for the dance tonight.
I hurt inside,
though I'd never let *them* know.
I make a face and ignore them,
but when they leave, I feel awful.
I know they're fools,
and I'm not what they say I am.
But it's so hard to feel good about yourself
when others point out your faults.
Can you understand why I'm crying, Lord?
And can't you make them stop?
Or at least make me strong enough to face them again?

▶ Do you ever need me, Lord?

It never occurred to me, God,
that you could use a friend from time to time.
It's most always been me asking you for
help with my personal problems.
And I haven't forgotten you are all powerful
and almighty, too.
But I like the idea that I could do
something for you—
like the special way I feel when I'm with
Grandpa.
He taught me how to fish and bait the hook
and clean the catch years ago.
Now when we go, he walks slower
leaning his hand on my shoulder as
we scale the hill to the dock.
I help him step into the boat,
and he lets me run the motor.
We're partners nowadays, he needs me
and I need him.
It makes me feel good.
So I'd like to promise, Lord,
if you need a partner,
you can lean on me.

Counting rainbows

I remember rainbows, Lord,
and places I've seen them.
I keep a count in my diary and
this afternoon's was the best yet!
A double arching set of rainbows
out over the lake.
First the dark clouds and rain
swirled the top of the water.
Then, as the sky began to clear,
it developed like a Polaroid snapshot,
brighter and clearer with each second.
Reds and purples, yellow, blue, and green,
hanging in midair.
And then a second one appeared above the first!
Sometimes I pretend I'm the only one seeing them,
and you're sending a special message just to me.
Rainbows twinkle with promises from you,
they say, "Don't worry, I'm near."
I remember rainbows,
I stop to watch them until they disappear,
and this afternoon's was the best yet.
Thank you, God, for painting promises in the sky
for all to see.

▶ Girlfriends with boyfriends

Oh God,
I need to have more patience, I think.
My best friend, Sue, has changed,
and I don't like it at all.
She never has time for us anymore,
she's worried about how she looks,
she's moody and only talks about her boyfriend.
I get so angry with her, and then
I feel guilty.
But really I'm jealous and
feeling neglected.
Now she goes to the movies with other couples,
and I'm left behind.
God, forgive me for being hard on her,
we've been friends since first grade,
nothing ever came between us until this.
Help me understand,
maybe I'd do the same thing, I don't know.
She doesn't know how I feel,
would you give me the courage to tell her?
I want to work at keeping her friendship,
and maybe adding some new ones, too.

For people with AIDS

Lord, I hear so much about AIDS
on the news, and in magazines.
Teachers talk about it,
parents worry over it,
famous stars and singers die from it,
and even little innocent babies
are born with it,
if their mom was a carrier.
It scares me, Lord,
will I get it too?
I can't imagine what it's like
to find you have only a year to live,
and there's no hope for cure—yet.
To know you'll lose weight
and have pain
and catch other viruses
is awful,
but the worst part must be
hearing people say, "you deserve it"
and having no one want to touch you.
No, I don't believe they deserve it
no matter how they got AIDS,
homosexuals,
drug users,
hemophiliacs,
children,
they all need our love.
I don't know anyone with AIDS,
but I pray I'd be kind to them if I did.
I know if I ever got it,

I'd need friends and family close by,
to be there for me.
Lord, be with those people who suffer,
and help us find a cure,
so that the pain will stop.

▶ What will you do about the animals?

Dear God, will you have room for animals in heaven, too?
We say we believe in the life of the world to come,
and it doesn't seem fair that you'd
make me live forever without
my good friend, Dublin.
I used to think she'd always be here,
lying under the desk in my room,
barking for her dinner at five o'clock,
staring at me from across the room
with her watery brown eyes.
But this year she moves a lot slower,
and limps when she first gets up.
She's full of lumps, her eyes are cloudy, and
her face is gray.
We're just the same age,
she's lived with Mom and Dad as long as I have.
I pray that you'll watch over her
and keep her safe.
And when we have to say good-bye, and I hope it's not too soon,
I know you'll take good care of her.
She likes to take long walks in the morning,
and she won't need a leash.
She'd be just about the best dog
you'd ever want.
I know you love her
like I do.
I know you love all your creatures

and want them to live with you forever.
I just have to believe you won't forget
Dublin in your plans.

▶ Fresh snow in the morning

The morning is full of magic,
God, snow was one of your best inventions!
The dull, brown grass is a white woolen carpet
that sparkles in the sun.
The branches are balancing a full inch of snow,
the fence posts too,
and the roof of the old birdfeeder out back.
The world is brighter,
the air is clearer, and
people are friendlier
when they pull on boots to shovel their walk.
I love the sound of clean snow
crunching underfoot
and the chance to step into freshly
dusted fields
before anyone but rabbits and birds
have left a trail.
I'm glad everyone has to stay home!
No school,
no work,
we're snowbound!
I think this is a perfect day you've made.
I feel good inside and out.
Thank you for this beautiful first snowfall,
and this morning full of winter magic.

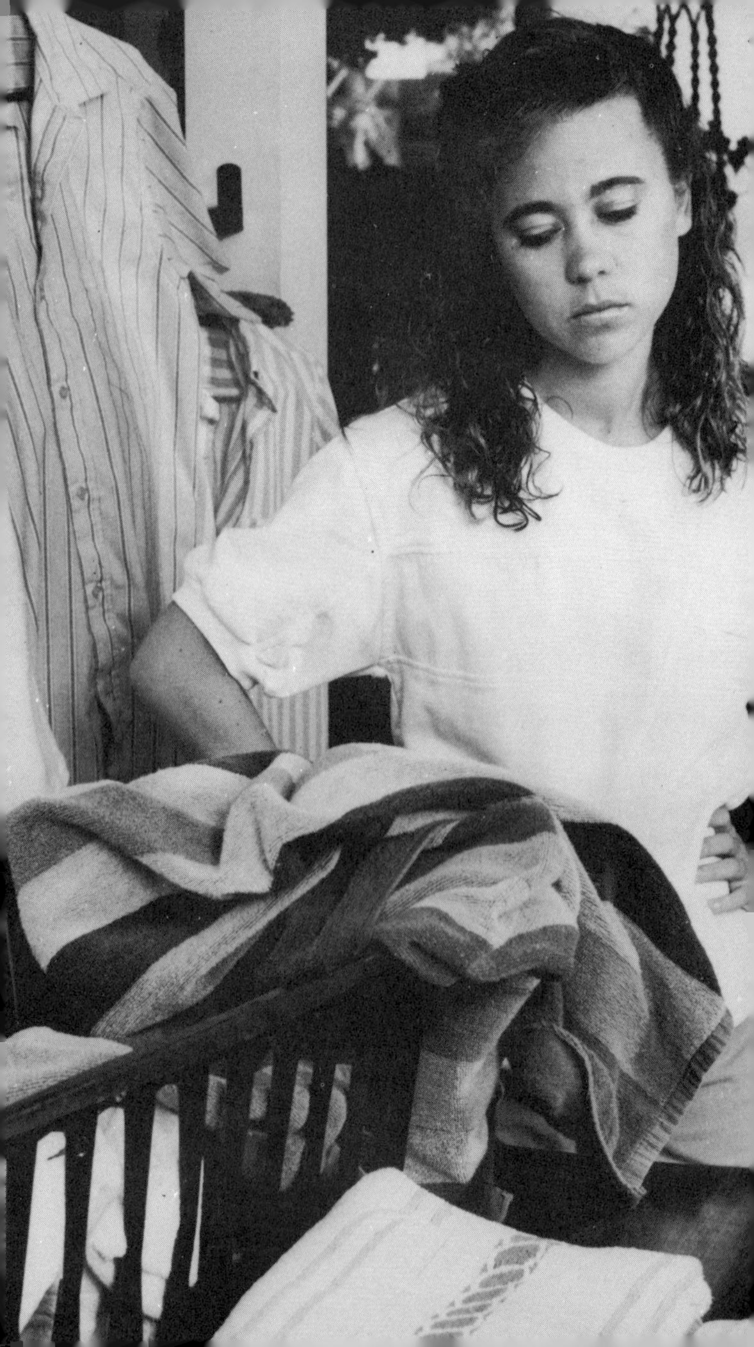

I don't mean to be rude

I'll have to admit, Lord, I'm feeling awful.
Lately my temper just flares up
and explodes like a volcano when Mom and I disagree.
I never did that before,
I used to want her to know what I was doing,
to see what I'd made in school,
to hear what the teachers said about my assignments.
I'm sorry that my words hurt her,
I didn't mean what I said,
it just came out before I could think.
Forgive me, Jesus,
forgive me for always thinking I'm right
and parents are always in the way.
You understand, don't you,
that I really want things to be like they used to be?
I don't like to fight
and to feel a cold silence in the house.
I love her, Lord, and I wasn't kind.
Help me to respect her feelings,
I want to apologize,
to try again.
I'm glad you understand
and that you love me even when I'm wrong.

▶ Am I an awful person?

My face burns where he hit me, Lord,
I can see the finger marks on my cheek.
I feel so empty inside,
so sad
and alone.
I don't understand why my boyfriend
gets so angry with me.
I like to think I'm special,
that he is proud to be with me,
at the movies and the football games.
He used to send me notes in class
and buy me little things,
flowers, a teddy-bear, or a bracelet,
for no reason at all.
Then it all changed.
Did I become an awful person, Jesus?
He says I don't listen
and I'm flirting with other guys.
And sometimes he throws me down,
and I'm afraid he'll hurt me.
You said, "turn the other cheek,"
but you didn't mean this for me.
I need the courage to leave him.
I need to know I'm a good person
and I deserve better.
Set me free from him, Lord,
I want to run to you
and feel your gentle, loving arms
keep me safe from all of this.
Hold me, Jesus, hold me.

▶ **It's too much!**

Tell me what to do, Jesus!
You always know what God wants,
can you tell me what to do first?
Who or what is most important in my life?
There are so many demands,
I'm ripping into a thousand pieces.
I'm torn
and tired.
Dad wants to see me for dinner tonight, because
it's his turn to visit.
But I have two tests tomorrow
and play practice.
There's dance lessons three times a week,
and my boyfriend wants me at the game Friday.
Mom thinks she's nothing more than my
taxi-driver,
and I can't miss another rehearsal for choir.
The dog needs her bath
and the lady next door wants me to babysit.
It's just too much, Lord!
I know I like to do so many things,
but I can't keep this up.
I'm only one person.
Is this what it means to grow up?
So many choices
and pressures?
I'm in no hurry, so
help me slow down.
Jesus, sort through these things
one by one,

I'll share the load with you.
Help me do what I can,
and remind me it doesn't depend on
　my strength alone.
I have you to see me through.

▶ Today I won't ask for anything

God is great and God is good,
and today I don't want anything special.
I don't want to remind you
to look out for my friends,
or to heal somebody,
or to give me courage.
Today I just want to say "Thank you,"
for those things that make life warm:
flannel sheets and woodburning stoves,
mugs of hot chocolate and candlelight.
There are things that brighten my day:
sunshine on my desk,
a phone call for me,
the beat of my favorite song,
my dog's frantic tail wagging.
O Lord, when you made the world,
you saw that it was good
and you filled it with colors:
peaceful sky blue and budding spring green,
lemon yellow and cranberry red.
And you gave me eyes to see mountains,
and ears to hear rushing streams,
and a heart to love my family and friends!
Thanks, God, for feelings,
for silly moods and serious worries,
for love and anger,
confusion and celebration,
and for days when I remember
to stop to count my blessings.
Thank you!

I got an "A"!

Oh, Lord it feels so good!
I was afraid to look
when she handed back the term papers.
I know I'm more than just a
list of grades on a report card,
but still it feels great to see "excellent"
written on something I've done!
Thank you, Spirit, for pushing me along
when I felt like quitting,
for tempting me to trust my instincts
and write about what matters to me.
English was always hard for me,
you know that . . .
but I wanted to prove I could do it!
I got an "A"
and I feel like I could
tackle the world!
C'mon, Lord, help me work on geography next!
We're on a roll!

The man on the steps

I love trips,
it's exciting to be in a new city,
to see new sights.
It's a treat to sleep on the floor
in the church that hosts our youth group each year.
For me, Jesus, it was fun for a night
to rough it.
The floor was hard,
and though I was chilly,
I loved the sound of rain on the roof.
But in the morning,
we all found Josh,
huddled on the front steps
outside the church.
He was shivering in the rain,
under a pink blanket,
like a stray dog.
It was so sad to see a grown man
with a stuffed animal for company.
His suitcase was out on the sidewalk open,
clothes scattered.
It felt so good to help,
to offer him hot coffee and breakfast.
How spoiled I am, Lord!
I have so much,
a home and family who cares,
food every day, and friends who listen.
I don't have to wander from doorstep to doorstep
like Josh,
looking for a home,

for someone to take me in.
He was so grateful for so little,
I wanted to give him so much more.
"God bless you!" he smiled,
clutching the Styrofoam cup with scabby hands.
You've given me so much,
this morning I pray you'd please bless Josh
with the feeling that someone cares.
And remember him, Lord, tonight when it gets dark
   and cold,
and keep him safe.
Help me remember him, too.

I hate smoke

Dear God,
my father is a smart man,
but he won't stop smoking.
And he won't listen to me
when I say I'm afraid
that he'll get cancer
like old Uncle Jack.
I watch him read the newspaper
and slowly reach for the pack
and puff
and inhale
until the room is gray
and adrift in smoke.
He tells me not to worry,
but I can't help it.
I love him so much
I don't ever want to see him
in a hospital,
sick and dying.
Please set your Spirit to work on him,
make him hear the family's concern.
Help him see that I love him and
that's why I bug him about this.
And God, I'll keep praying for him
even if he doesn't like it,
until we make him stop.
In the meantime,
please keep him healthy
and give me the faith to hang in there.

▶ An old friend's voice

I have to laugh, Lord,
it made me smile and remember
so many neighborhood events
when Wendy called today.
Old friends are so special,
they're like seashells,
filled with the sounds of younger days.
I hadn't talked to her in a year,
but I always recognize her voice.
We had such fun in grade school.
We learned to ride bikes the same month,
and we took swimming lessons at the pool.
She'd invite me for dinner once a week
and I'd bring her on our vacations.
We cried when she moved because
we were inseparable.
I feel older, Lord, when we talk now,
it's a different time,
and I have new friends.
But I'll always want to remember
my old friends
and the memories only we can share.
I hope I'm a good friend, Lord, but
I know you're the best friend of all.
You'll never forget me,
and you'll never move away!

Dancing for peace

Lord, I have an idea.
You know I love music,
the rhythm and beat,
it makes me want to jump up and move
and dance.
When the song starts to pulse,
it fills my head,
and I forget what I've been worrying about,
I let it all go and
get lost in the music.
Thanks God, for dancing,
it makes people laugh and clown,
it makes them work the bad stuff out
of their system.
So I was wondering,
if we want world peace,
why summit conferences must be so serious?
Why don't we have a dance for the leaders
when they come?
A dance with a great beat for the Russians
and the Arabs.
Let the South Africans get lost in the music,
and forget their worries,
and move together
without stepping on each other's toes,
and work the bad stuff out of their systems.
Lord, it's worth a try!
Give us peace, in Jesus' name.

▶ A walk in the woods

Lord, sometimes there is so much noise
in my day,
school bells ringing
and cars honking,
the roar of the malls,
and the bickering of my friends.
When I feel uptight and confused,
like a rocket about to begin countdown,
then come to me, Lord, and
walk with me into the woods.
I need to hear the simpler sounds
of squirrels scolding from the treetops
and chickadees singing.
Sometimes I believe your Spirit comes to me,
in the gentle whisper of the wind between the leaves
and the movement of wispy clouds overhead.
I see your brush strokes in the purple and rose sunset,
and I start to relax
and smile inside.
Don't let me ever lose you, Lord,
or drown the welcome music of your voice
from my ears.
Thank you for the peace I find
when we walk in the stillness of the woods
and end our day together.

▶ It's embarrassing to ask questions

There are things I'm really curious about, Jesus.
I've had so many questions
about things I've always been told.
I never asked before
how you felt as a teenager.
Did you get impatient with Mary your mother,
like I do with mine?
Did you want to break the rules
and be on your own?
Did your friends make fun of your interest in religion
and call your ideas strange?
Jesus, did you feel just like me some days?
My pastor says you did,
but I want to ask more.
Like, how can you be God and human
both at the same time?
What was it like to rise from the dead,
and why after three days?
I wonder about my faith,
and I feel like you're reaching out to me
across a wide canyon,
and I want to reach back.
But I don't ask the questions, because
the class would tease and call me strange.
I'm torn.
I wish it didn't matter what they think.
I feel guilty because I desert you first
when the going gets tough,
like the disciple, Peter, who denied you three times.
I'm sorry for being so weak.

Help me to be myself in class,
to be curious and confident.
I'll get better, Jesus, with your help,
but today I'll ask the pastor my questions
after class,
and I won't be embarrassed.
I'll start reaching for your hand, Lord,
because I know you're waiting for me.

▶ What is it about boys?

Dear God, boys make me nervous!
Why are they so much different than girls?
They make me laugh at silly things,
and I worry how I look.
Is my hair just so
and my makeup OK?
I say the dumbest things
like I haven't any brains
when the one I like comes around.
I like to catch his eye
and feel him watching me.
Lord, what is it about boys
that makes me try so hard
to be noticed?
I try to be beautiful,
then I laugh too loud.
I say things I don't mean,
and I feel foolish afterwards.
Help me to work on being me,
with girls or with boys.
I don't need to play the part of someone else,
I want to trust who I am.
Deep inside
I sense your love.
I know I'm not silly or dumb,
and I don't have to try at all
to be noticed by you.

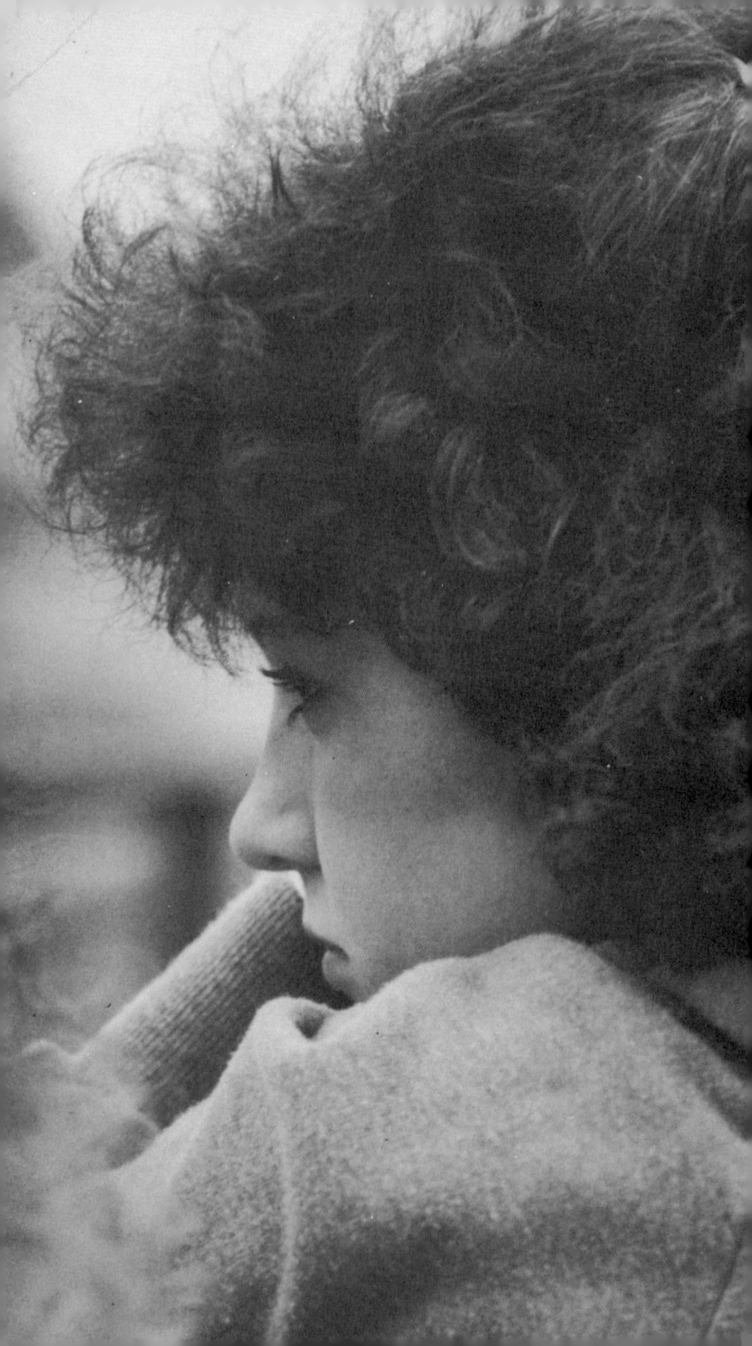

Never content

I think it's a problem, Lord,
to never be content with myself.
Mom's tired of hearing me complain,
and I wonder how it sounds to you
who gave each one of us a special gift
unlike anyone else's?
Too often I catch myself
wishing I had olive skin like my friend Sharon,
then I wouldn't be so pasty and pale.
I wish my hair was full and thick
like my cousin Sarah's
so I'd never need another perm.
I find Michelle's clothes nicer than mine,
and Rob is smarter in math.
Open my eyes, Lord, to my own strengths,
don't let me be like a child
who ungratefully ignores the gifts in front of her
while envying the packages everyone else receives.
You wrapped me in a strong body
with a creative mind
and what Mom calls a "bubbly" personality.
People like me,
and Rob likes me a whole lot.
I'm not so bad just the way I am, Lord.
Thank you!

▶ Helpless

Dear Jesus, I don't know what to do
to help my parents hurt less.
They walk around like they're made of glass
and will shatter at the slightest touch.
They seem frozen at times,
sitting in a daze at breakfast.
No one talks,
then mother will start to cry.
I want to say something
or show them something new to make them forget
that my brother is gone.
When you lose someone, Jesus,
you feel so helpless.
The pain makes people crazy,
and it's hard just to watch,
but I don't know what to do.
And I'm sorry to be angry at my brother
for not talking to me,
for not thinking of Mom and Dad.
I can't believe he did it.
I know I don't have to pick up the pieces,
but I feel that way.
Suicide is the most awful way
to hurt the ones you love.
Jesus, I believe death isn't the end, and
I know I'll see my brother again.
But please help us now.
Heal my parents' aching hearts
and mine, too,
and tell my brother we miss him.

Baby-sitting

God, don't you think I'll make a great mother?
Babies like me,
I can make them giggle and smile
and eat their supper,
and I can change diapers in a flash.
I like to feel in charge,
to know I'm the only one in the house
and the kids have to listen to *me* for once!
I can say no to things they
shouldn't do
and teach them the names for
things they'll have to know.
And Lord, when I'm with children,
then I feel responsible,
older, and grownup,
and I like that.
I make my own decisions, and
no one tells me what to do every minute,
because they trust my judgment.
It doesn't seem like work
when you do something that comes naturally.
It's just plain fun!

▶ I made the team

Oh, thank you, Lord!
I made the team!
I've been hoping and praying
for so long that I could
play on the varsity team,
but the other girls looked so good,
I never dreamed I could qualify.
This means I'll be one of them,
I can travel and compete, and
I'll have a jersey and a number
of my own!
Oh, God, it feels good to be chosen,
to know the coach thinks I'm OK,
showing promise,
a great addition to the line-up.
I'm going to give it my best shot.
I worked hard to make it, Lord,
I practiced and ran and ran again.
And you know what?
It was all worth it
to see my name on the bulletin board this morning.
I can't wait for practice to begin.
I made the team!

A guest in my own homes

Two homes are one too many, Jesus.
At first it was exciting
to have two rooms,
one with mom and
a new one in my dad's apartment.
He'd buy me almost anything I want,
new curtains and my own desk,
new lamps and a blue rug.
But I'm tired of traveling back and forth,
of watching my parents compete for my attention.
Everything's so mixed up,
I don't know where to settle in,
so I live like a guest in my own home.
My stepsister is a pain,
she tries to distract my dad and
make my stepmother angry with me.
I'm tired of the whole scene.
I just want to unpack my suitcase
and put it away for good.
I pray for your guidance, Jesus, because
I want to stop this merry-go-round.
You know what it's like,
to have a home with us on earth
and another with God in heaven.
It's so hard wanting to please everyone,
loving both parents,
and needing time with each one.
But I have to choose one place to live.
Help me, Lord, so they'll understand,
and so I can find peace.

▶ Waiting for the school bus

Oh, Lord, some days the bus takes forever!
It's awful to stand here by myself,
hoping the boys won't bother me,
that they won't make smart remarks
about the coat I wear,
or the books I carry.
They push each other around,
wrestle, and
throw apples at one another.
I just wish I could disappear,
and not have to worry every day,
about the kids on the corner
and how I'll survive the 10 minute wait.
The girls are no better,
they huddle in a group and giggle,
and whisper and make it clear,
I'm not one of them.
It feels so alone, Lord,
are they afraid of me
like I am of them?
Come with me this morning,
and make me strong enough
to face them again.

I can't help it

Jesus, I like a challenge.
I like it when someone says that I can't:
that I can't run faster,
or win the game,
or make the grade,
because I want to show them I can.
I feel a rush of excitement
when the contest begins
and I give it my all,
and I come out ahead.
I don't like to be predictable, Jesus.
I don't want to hear "girls can't do that"
just because they never have.
I like to try new things,
and to compete with boys and girls,
and to push myself.
They say I threaten the boys,
that I should hold back and not
try to keep up,
but I can't help it.
I don't want to boast or brag,
I just like a challenge
and the freedom to be all I can be.
You came to set us free,
not to keep women in their place,
and I like that!

Two sides of me

Jesus, I want to be a good person,
a respectful student the teachers enjoy,
a successful leader,
and smart.
That's a side of me I know well,
and I'm proud to get recognition
and awards for doing what is expected.
Yet I think there's another part of me,
a side I don't talk about much,
but you know it's there.
Sometimes I find it boring to be good,
and I sense a wild streak
trying to break out.
I think about skipping class
and going to the beach with my friends.
I wonder what it'd be like to flunk a test,
to drink a bottle of wine,
to get high on coke,
to sneak out of the house
after midnight
and drive around town.
There is a side to me that scares me
and tempts me to do the unexpected,
to take a risk and dare myself to do
what I know is wrong.
There are times I'm afraid
I'll just give in
and I'll be sorry.
Jesus, I know you were tempted too,
and you don't blame me for having two sides.

I know I'm capable of doing wonderful things,
and I know I can also do terrible things.
I pray you'll guide me through those tempting
   moments
and help me resist hurting myself and others.
It's not easy, Jesus, to do what's right,
I need all the support you can give.

Timeless

How old are you, God?
They say you are timeless,
with no beginning and no end.
I can't imagine that,
to live before you were born
and to know you'll never age!
I know you're older than 1,000 years
and even more than 10,000,
but to say you're as old as forever
is too hard to understand.
I sometimes get bored when I have
a night with nothing to do,
but what's one Saturday night
to you?
How many Saturdays have you seen?
And how many summer vacations?
Do you cross off days on a calendar
like I do,
and tell time on a clock?
How can you keep track of so many years
and so many birthdays
for all of your children?
When I really think about it, Lord,
it's amazing
that you'll take time to listen
to one little teenage girl
like me.

Please talk to my parents

Oh, Lord, please talk to my parents!
You could make them relax
and not worry so much about me.
I feel like I can't move.
I'm suffocating in the house
with the rules and curfews
they list for me.
"Don't do this," and "Be careful,"
"I don't like your friends,"
and "That's too dangerous."
I try to do what they want,
but sometimes it's just too hard.
Tell them I'm going to be all right
if I go to the mall with my friends,
and tell them I'll survive
a trip to the big city.
Can you make them trust
that I don't do drugs,
and I'm not drinking at parties,
and my boyfriend is not really wild?
I don't understand why they're so afraid
when I've never done anything
so terribly wrong.
Jesus, you know I have nothing to hide,
yet my parents are so suspicious of me.
Talk to them, please,
and tell them they don't have to try
so hard to be good parents.
I'll be OK,
and they don't have to worry.

I can't keep up

Oh Lord, you know school
isn't my best subject!
I'm just not a student
who can breeze into a test
without studying the night before.
I can't always understand
what I read the first time through.
My friends aren't any help, Lord,
and I get angry when they tease me
and make fun of my questions.
I do so much pretending.
Pretending that I can
get my homework done and join
my friends at a party, too.
I lied about my grades to them and
told them I wasn't worried
when I was scared to death.
I just can't keep up with them,
and I'm miserable trying.
I'm sorry, Jesus, for being false
and too proud to level with
myself and my friends.
I need to learn at my own pace
and ask for the help it takes.
I'm no dummy, I'll show 'em!
It just takes me a little longer,
and that's OK, too.
Help me take the time necessary, Lord,
with no apologies!

Letting things slide

Something's not right, Lord,
I'm letting things slide right by.
Deadlines for tests, papers' due dates
wash over me, and I don't care.
Jesus, this isn't like me,
I'm not usually so lazy
and uninspired to do my work.
Seeing my friends doesn't help either,
they say I'm no fun,
because I don't want to do anything.
I feel like I'm sinking down into sticky mud,
and I'm too tired to lift my feet.
I'm scared, Jesus.
I don't know why I'm so sad,
and I just want to be alone.
I've started to drink, because
then I feel relaxed and I don't worry.
No one knows but you,
and I know you don't approve.
Help me stop.
I'm not sure I like what's happening.
I'm sorry, but it's getting out of control,
and my secret will be discovered soon.
I need to talk to someone,
guide me to the right one.
I know you'll stick with me.
I'm not a bad person,
things just got a little out of hand.
I don't want to sink any deeper,
grab my hand, Lord, and pull me out.

A candle flame

A friend once told me, Lord,
to light a candle
in my room
when I'm alone and want to
spend time in prayer;
time getting in touch with you.
The glowing gold flame
reminds me that your Spirit is
bright and warm,
and it moves here and there
with the wind.
There is something special
about those moments I spend in my room,
a mystery in the silence,
and I always hope you will speak to me.
I know you spoke to Moses from
a burning bush
and led his people by a pillar of fire.
Lord, I imagine as I stare at the candle
that you have some great assignment for me,
like one of the prophets in the Bible!
I like the feeling
that we have a close relationship
although I never see you.
Even though you don't talk out loud
from the trembling flame,
I know you're here,
and I feel your touch.

Broken promises

O God, what can I do?
I'm so angry with myself,
so sick of saying I'll lose weight
and I never do.
I hate my legs,
I look awful in pants,
and I'm embarrassed in gym class.
The teacher looks at me,
I know she wants to shake her head
and say, "How did she let herself get so big?"
I've heard it all before, Lord,
"no snacks," "no between meal snacks,"
"start exercising."
I'm going to change this time.
I will not cheat on my diet.
I'll walk every day to school,
in the rain and the snow,
and I won't give in this time.
You gave me as much self-control as the next girl,
and I'm promising myself,
not my gym teacher, or my parents,
that this time
I'll do it!
This time, I feel I'm angry enough,
and if you'll help me,
they won't call me "fat" anymore!

▶ Dad's out of work

Dear God, my dad needs your help.
I think he's hurting pretty bad
since the factory laid him off,
and he's been trying to find another job.
I feel so sorry for him, because
it wasn't his fault they closed the plant.
He doesn't think we understand, Lord,
but we do.
I tell him I love him,
and it doesn't matter that he can't
afford to buy me things I want right now.
I don't care about that,
but he doesn't seem to believe me.
He's being too hard on himself,
and he feels guilty and worthless.
Lift his load of care,
so he can see that Mom, my brother, and I love him.
I believe he'll find work soon.
Won't you tell him to have a little faith, too?

I want a date

Jesus, I hope you understand
that just about more than anything
I want a date.
I want a boy to invite me to the dance
or treat me to the movies.
I'd like to have him pass me notes,
and smile at me in the lunch room,
and wait for me outside of class.
The girls are OK for most days,
but on weekends,
just now and then,
I'd like to have a boyfriend
who's wild about me,
who'd invite me out to exciting places.
Lord, sometimes I feel like I'm
the only one of my friends who
still hasn't had a boyfriend.
I like plenty of guys,
and I try to pretend they like me,
but it's a game I play alone.
Jesus, I want to be loved.
You know what I mean, don't you?
Mom says my time will come,
to relax and stop worrying about it.
Help me, Lord,
it's so hard to wait!

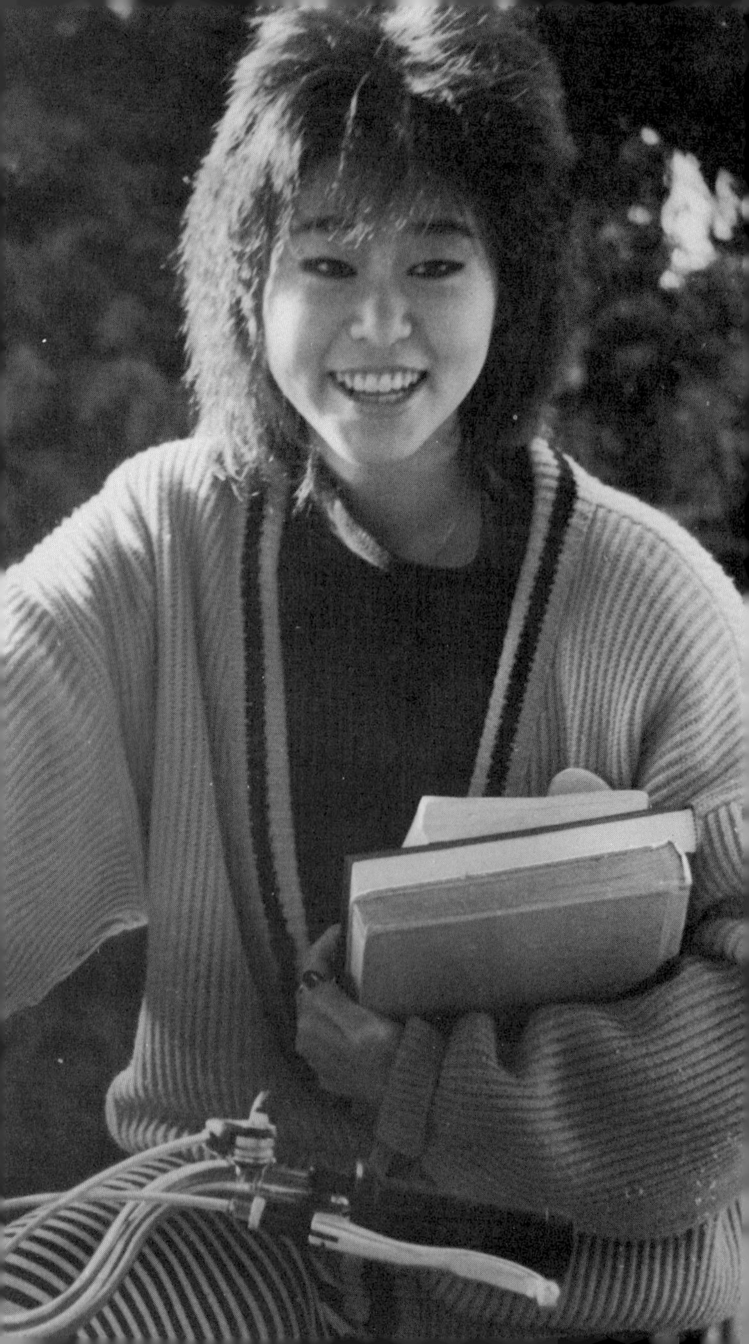

When I'm a woman

Dear God,
when I'm a woman,
I think I'd like to be
a drama coach, like Ms. Stearns.
I love to watch her
read the lines of our play
so confidently.
She feels what she says
and acts so naturally.
I'd like to know as much as she does
about Shakespeare and Tennessee Williams.
I'd love to go to Broadway
with her
and be able to critique the production
and carry on an intelligent conversation.
Lord, will I ever be a good actress,
and be able to move the audience
to tears by the convincing performance
I gave?
Ms. Stearns sees so much in each line,
in each scene.
I want to learn all I can from her,
to soak up all she can tell me!
I wonder, Lord, are you calling me to the stage?
Is this what you want me to do?
I hope so, because,
Ms. Stearns says I'm good
and I show great promise!

I'll do it later

Jesus, when will I learn
not to wait until the last minute
to start to get ready?
It's always the same,
for tests or reports due,
for recitals, the dishes,
washing my hair,
ironing my blouse for morning.
"I'll do it later,"
is my favorite line.
Lord, I get so angry with myself,
and I know I drive my parents nuts.
I mean to take myself by the arm
and say "do it now!"
Then I start to clean my desk
or walk the dog, and
I think of a hundred things I should do first.
Push me, Jesus,
pull me away from all the distractions
and make me change my ways,
'cause I'm so weak.
Help me plan ahead
and stop putting things off.
I want to show them,
I can be organized, self-disciplined,
and finish *early* for once!

▶ Mom's getting married

Lord Jesus,
I should be happy for Mom, because
she's found a man to love,
and he loves her, too.
They don't fight like
she did with Dad,
and my little brother
is crazy about him.
But, Jesus, I'm not.
I know Dad's not coming back,
but I don't like seeing Mom with another man.
I guess I'm jealous for Dad
and for the way it used to be,
when all of us were together.
And I think I liked it better
when Mom had more time for me,
and wasn't so busy with him.
I can't call him "Dad,"
and I'm not sure I'll like him living here.
Lord, I'm all mixed up.
Being at your mother's wedding isn't easy,
and I don't want to make her unhappy.
I promise I'll try to get along.
I know it's hard for him,
coming to live with the three of us.
I just wish I could be happier
and not be jealous.
I pray that you'll help us become a family,
and give us patience with each other,
and love.

Honesty

Dear God,
I'm in such a mess!
I didn't have the nerve to tell them
why I didn't get home until midnight.
They'd just get upset
and give me one of those piercing,
disapproving looks
and another long lecture on boys and sex.
Oh Jesus, I'm sorry,
we left the party for a drive,
and I didn't want to tell him
I had to be home.
I was afraid he'd think I was too young,
and my parents' rules were too silly,
so I didn't care about the time.
But I feel uncomfortable inside,
and I avoid looking Mom in the eyes.
I think she suspects I'm lying,
and I never did that before.
We didn't do anything wrong, and
I really have nothing to hide,
except the lie I told.
I want my parents to trust me, and
I know you don't approve, Jesus,
of sneaking around behind their backs.
Forgive me.
I don't want to hurt them.
I'll tell them the truth,
and I hope we all feel better.
Give me the courage!

▶ Love is a big feeling

Jesus, how do you know you're in love?
When I think of love,
I think of a feeling that lasts forever.
I picture a home and children
and a man who thinks I'm the best wife
in the world.
To be in love means you like the same guy
this week and next week
and years and years later,
even when he makes you mad
and you work long hours
and get tired and argue.
Love is a big enough feeling
to bring you through those hard days.
Lord, when I think about all of that,
I don't really love my boyfriend, do I?
We've been together a month,
and I'm already bored with him.
I saw another guy at the dance
who was looking at me.
He's awfully cute, and
I'd like to get to know him, too.
Jesus, I don't think I'm ready for love.
Someday I want to be,
but not now!
I'm too young to get serious, because
there's plenty of time.
But, Lord, let me know when it's the real thing!

▶ Were parents ever teenagers?

Lord, I wonder if parents
were ever really young?
It seems they can't remember
what good music sounds like
or why it has to be heard
while I'm reading
and writing
and showering
and cleaning my room.
If they were once teenagers,
why don't they understand
I need time away from them
without them hovering over me
and asking a hundred questions?
Why aren't they laughing when
I tell them how we teased the teacher today
and I got detention,
and when I remind them that algebra will
be of no use to me
when I'm a famous lawyer one day?
Jesus, when I get older,
I hope I don't forget the many feelings
I had as a kid.
Please give my parents a better memory
and a little sense of humor, Lord.
They take everything so seriously, including me.
I'm grateful for their concern, I suppose, because
that's part of being a parent.
I know they love me,
but can't you make them more fun?

I'm no quitter

Dad called me a "quitter" today
and it hurt.
I'm tired of losing the games,
tired of coming in second
or third.
I'm no quitter.
I've practiced and done the drills
over and over,
but when the tournament begins,
I get so nervous and
I lose my concentration.
The coach says he'll work with me.
Oh Lord, I'm afraid I can't change!
I want to win,
to smash a serve right by her,
run to the net and put every shot away.
Lord, I need a second wind,
send me your Spirit to give me hope again
and courage to believe I can win.
Dad is wrong.
I won't stop trying yet, Lord, if you
work with me and
stay by me.
Help me forget the past
and look to the next match!

Life was so easy

Dear Jesus,
I feel like I'm living a bad dream.
I want to wake up and
have all the pills,
hospital visits, and
chemotherapy vanish
like smoke in the wind.
Life was so easy when
Mom was healthy.
I never had to worry about
anything but homework
and going to the mall.
Jesus, now I feel so old.
I'm afraid Mom won't get over
this cancer,
but I try to tell her
she'll be all right.
Lord, you healed so many cripples
and people with diseases.
Will you please remember my Mom?
She's so weak and weary.
Won't you take away her pain
and kill this tumor, so
she can act like her old self again?
I'm so afraid to lose her.
She's too young to die,
and we need her so.
More than anything,
please make her well,
and be with Dad.

We won't give up hope,
because we know
you're here with us.

▶ When to stop?

God, I've been avoiding you,
and I'm sorry.
But I was embarrassed to talk
about this,
and sometimes I don't really
want to know what your will is for me,
'cause I think I'll have to stop.
Oh, God, I'm having such fun,
I never knew kissing could be
so exciting!
I love to hug and hold hands
and my boyfriend is so good to me.
Is it wrong, Lord?
It feels good, even though
at first we were nervous,
but not anymore.
But, Lord, when do we stop?
And who is in charge—
do I say no or should he?
As it gets more comfortable,
we talk about going farther,
but I can tell that would be wrong.
Lord, help us set limits
and to be wise and respect
one another's bodies.
It's so hard to stop,
and so difficult to talk about this.
Give us the courage to say no,
because we really care for each other,
and because we love you.

Faith like his

Oh Lord,
I hate seeing Grandpa this way.
I held his hand;
it was warm and smooth.
He lay in the hospital bed
and he never spoke
or opened his eyes.
I missed his smile,
the way his face crinkled up, and
how he'd bend down to kiss me.
Dad said Grandpa knew I was there
when I felt him squeeze back
as I whispered in his ear,
"Please get well!"
Lord, I thought of one thing he
always used to say
as I watched his face,
memorizing wrinkles
and the shape of his nose.
We talked about life and love
and plants when we worked in the garden.
But more than anything else,
he'd say, "I'm not afraid to die,
'cause I know my Lord's waitin' for me."
I'm so glad he said that to me, Jesus,
especially today,
when he is so silent.
Grandpa has so much faith.
I hope a little rubbed off on me,
so that when I must say good-bye,

I won't be afraid,
because I know he's a good man,
and you've been waiting for him
for a long time.

▶ Do something for Sarah

Lord Jesus,
you've just got to help
my friend Sarah.
I don't know where she went,
but her mom thinks I know.
She's run away, Lord,
I'm sure of it.
I don't blame her,
the way she gets treated
by her stepfather.
She doesn't trust him.
One minute he'll be really nice
and then the next he'll
scream and yell
and even hit her.
Jesus, why should she have
to come to school with black eyes
and say she had an accident?
She asked me not to tell,
made me promise,
but I think it's gone too far.
Keep her safe.
Let her know you love her, Lord, because
she doesn't have much at home.
I want to do the right thing for her.
I want the fighting and anger to stop
before she gets badly hurt.
Lord, it's not fair to her,
she's a good friend.
I hope she'll forgive me

for talking to my mom.
I don't know what else to do
but I can't do it alone,
whatever we decide.
Show her we won't let her down,
if she needs a friend or two.
She's got me,
and I hope she believes
she's got you.

▶ My friend doesn't believe

I never knew anyone
who didn't believe in you, Lord.
And it's really strange
to try and convince someone
that I believe in something
I can't prove,
like a calculus equation
or a formula for chemistry.
I tell her it's like trusting someone,
to always be on your side,
to have an open ear
and a lot of love to share.
Lord, that's what you are to me,
but is that enough to change her mind?
I pray that something I say or do
will make a difference to her.
I'd like her to come to church with me,
to hear that Christ died for her sins
and that he sets us free to love everyone
as a child of God.
I need patience,
the right timing,
and maybe more faith
that you will work through me
to reach my skeptical friend.
Help me to trust in your Spirit
and in your time, Lord.
We don't have to hurry.

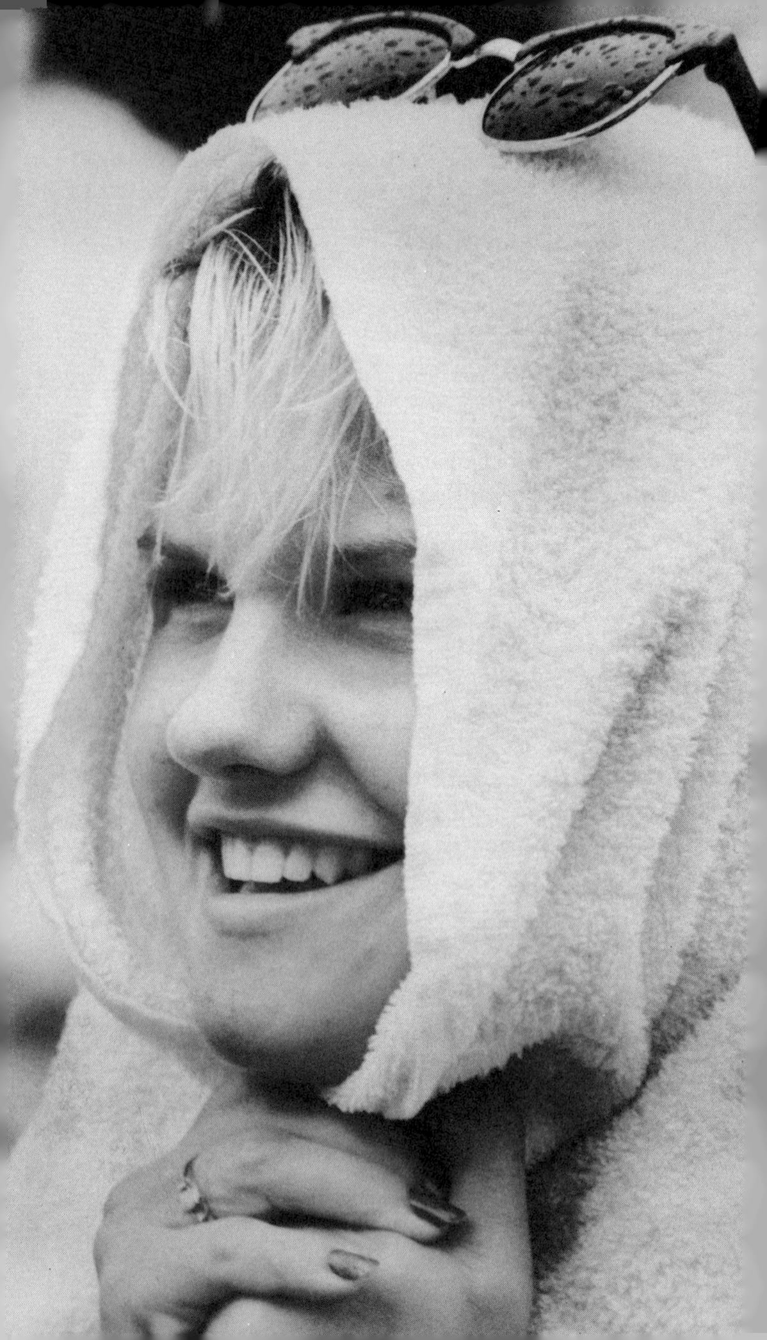

▶ What do you look like?

It's been said a lot lately
that you're not all male
or all female, God,
but perhaps both,
or neither, I'm not sure.
I try to picture
what a spirit looks like—
white like puffy clouds,
or thin and gray like fog?
I suppose it doesn't matter, because
it's really your business
how you look and what you are.
But sometimes when I pray,
I try to picture your face
looking warm and gentle as a mother,
and strong and firm as a father.
Then I give up
and decide I'll have to wait
and see you face to face at the end.
I hope you're not offended, but
I was just curious.
You did bless me with a brain
full of questions.
Thanks for listening, Lord.

▶ Why me?

It's happened again, Jesus,
I'm doing all the work.
No matter what committee
I volunteer for,
I end up in charge of all the details.
Why don't the others
do their part?
It would sure be easier,
and I wouldn't get so angry
and uptight.
Am I doing something wrong,
insisting on my way,
making the others feel inadequate?
If so, Lord,
I'm sorry.
I want us to work as a team,
have fun,
and plan together.
Maybe it's me.
My teacher says I like to
be in control.
I guess I blew it;
it had to be my way
or nothing at all.
Forgive me and teach me to let go a bit,
help me share the work
and trust others can follow through.
In your name, I pray.

How can you top this?

Oh God, I'm so happy I want to scream!
It's the first day of summer vacation
and the world's blooming and budding
and turning five shades of green everywhere.
My tests are over,
my grades are super,
I may have a summer job;
what more could I ask?
Lord, they say heaven is too good
to be true,
a paradise forever,
but things are so good here today,
I'm not sure heaven can top this!
The tulips are open,
the dogwoods are blooming,
and lilacs are getting ready
to scent the backyard.
And I have all day
to do what I want,
when I want,
under a clear blue sky.
Thank you, God, it's a perfect day!

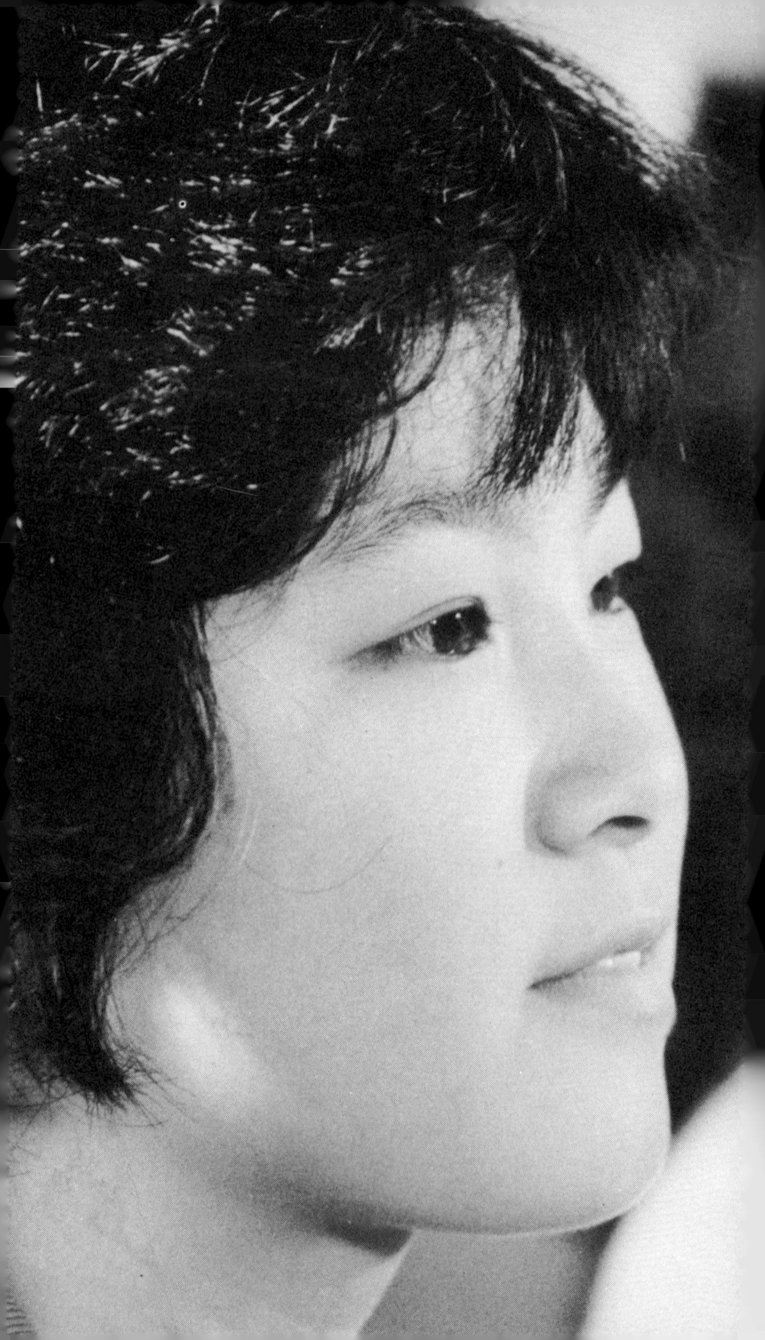

▶ What's wrong with people?

I have no right to ask, Jesus,
because I know I'm no angel,
but what's wrong with people?
I heard on the news about parents
who beat their little child
until it lost consciousness
and died.
That was *this* time.
The reporter said the child
had been burned
and sometimes starved.
I can't believe those things
are true, Lord.
How can it be happening?
I tried to imagine what it was like,
to be so small and helpless
and to suffer so much.
I couldn't.
I'm afraid I'll have bad dreams
about this
because I can't stop thinking about it.
Jesus, people can be so cruel
to one another,
I wish you could stop all this abuse.
I wish all children were safe
in their homes
and had parents who loved them.
People were cruel to you, Lord, when
they beat you and nailed you to a cross.
You died to change all this violence,

didn't you, Jesus?
I guess some never got the message.
I pray they will someday soon,
for the sake of the little children
who can't protect themselves.

The train

Lord, when I'm all snuggled down
under my comforter at night,
I love to hear the hollow whistle
of the train
and the clicking of the cars
across the tracks.
It's a regular sound
at 20 minutes past the hour,
a familiar sound I rarely notice.
Still, tonight, Lord,
I wonder what it would be like
to jump the train at midnight
and travel somewhere new?
I'm bored with this same old town,
the same old neighbors,
and the same old cracks in the sidewalk
on the way to the bus.
I've seen the hobos in the movies
jump aboard a train and ride west
to the mountains
or the coast.
I've never seen the Atlantic Ocean
or snow on top of the Rockies.
I'd like to see a desert
and some cactus in bloom.
I'm crazy, I suppose, just dreaming, because
I know the train goes three more stops
and turns around to head to the city again.
I want to travel, Lord,
when I hear the sound of the train,

and I pray my dreams will come true.
Good night . . .
I'm too comfortable to go anywhere
right now!

▶ Not eating enough

I've seen her
and heard her in the bathroom.
O God, it's so disgusting.
She tries to throw up
after lunch,
and I don't get it.
She says she's too heavy,
her pants are tight,
and her stomach isn't flat.
Jesus, I'm worried about Jen,
she's thin as a twig now.
She's obsessed with her weight
and constantly asks me if I think
she's gross or
too big.
Whatever I say doesn't stop her, because
she keeps on binging and vomiting.
I know that's not normal,
and it's not good for you.
I'll break our secret
if I go and tell her mom,
but I'm afraid if I don't,
something terrible will happen.
The Bible says that our bodies
are the temple of the Holy Spirit,
and we should honor them.
Jen is wrong.
What she's doing is wrong.
Please tell her she's thin enough
and make her listen to us

before she really gets sick.
Take care of my friend, Lord,
she's very special to me.

An accident

When I say in church
"I believe in the resurrection
of the dead, and the life everlasting,"
I thought it was for old people.
It's something old people count on,
because they're going to die soon.
I thought young kids like me
never had to worry—
until this week.
Mark sat next to me in algebra
on Wednesday,
he was wearing a red plaid shirt,
and I remember the joke he told me.
His older brother picked him up after school,
and a truck ran a red light at some intersection.
Mark was killed.
The words sound so foreign,
it must be a mistake.
I never knew anyone who died before, especially
no one close to me.
I can't stop crying
at lunch and in the halls,
and especially in algebra class
when I see the empty desk next to me.
He's just sick, Lord, isn't he?
He'll be back tomorrow, right?
It's too crazy to be true.
Why? Why did this happen?
Yesterday he made me laugh,
and we talked about the weekend.

I hate this, Lord, because I feel so sad,
so shocked.
Where were you when Mark needed you?
Why did the truck run the light?
Why?

▶ Telling secrets

Jesus,
she told me I was a lousy friend, and
she hates me for telling Tim
her secrets.
She yelled and slammed the locker
and stormed off down the hall.
"I can't trust you,"
were her final words.
What if she's right, Lord?
What if I really am a loudmouth
rat of a friend
who just goes around betraying
others who count on me?
I'd never want that because
I didn't mean to hurt her.
I don't know why
I let Tim know her feelings.
I was wrong,
O, Jesus, and I feel so rotten.
She's never been this mad at me,
but I can't blame her.
If she did the same to me,
I'd be furious.
I'm sorry, Jesus,
forgive me.
She hurts,
and I hurt.
She can trust me,
you know she can.
Tell her I'm not so bad,

and I won't do it again.
I can be her good friend,
if she'll let me.

Sunday

Grandma says Sundays used to be different
when she was a girl.
"We knew how to keep the Sabbath holy!"
she reminds me, Lord.
The whole family went to church
and Sunday school together.
Then they had the big noon meal
with a roast and potatoes and
fresh baked bread.
"It was a day of rest,
not like Sundays nowadays."
Well, I go to church, too,
but I also go to the mall
and to the movies.
Some of my friends work,
and my sister has soccer games.
We rarely have a dinner at noon because
everyone's always running someplace.
Sunday doesn't seem much different than
any other day.
I'm sorry, Lord,
I think we've let you down.
I'd like to try the way Grandma remembers,
where everybody just stayed together
and ate and talked and played games.
Family time—that would be different!
A whole day when we didn't hurry to
piano lessons and soccer practice
or computer workshops,
a day when we paused to thank you

for all the blessings of the past week.
A day of rest,
as you intended, is what we truly need.

At odds

Dear God,
my dad thinks we need more
nuclear weapons
to insure world peace.
I think we need to use
all that money for missiles
to feed the poor instead.
Dad thinks I should go to college and
get a degree in business, but
I want to get into modeling
and fashion design.
He votes Republican,
and I like the Democratic candidates.
I like ballet
and he prefers football.
Lord, I wonder sometimes
what do Dad and I have in common?
I try to be patient,
hoping that the next time
we discuss an issue,
and I give my feelings on the subject,
he'll smile and say,
"You're so right!"
But he has to lecture,
point out my faulty reasoning,
and show me I'm wrong.
It wears me down,
and I don't feel like sharing my dreams
or any opinions with him anymore.
I'll keep them to myself,

unless
you'll help me find a way
to get along with him and stop arguing.
I'd prefer that,
just show me how, Lord,
and I'll try one more time.

When I get married

Dear Lord,
when I marry my husband,
we'll always be kind
to each other.
We'll leave for work
in the morning
with a hug and a kiss
and tell one another
about our day over dinner.
I want to be in love
with only him,
and laugh at his jokes,
buy him silly gifts,
and plan exotic vacations
in spring and fall.
When I marry,
I want it to last,
so my children will never
know how much it hurts
when your parents divorce
and one moves away.
The hard part is accepting
it'll never be the same,
and it wasn't your fault.
Lord, I don't ever want to go
through this again.
I want to be happy.
Help me find the way.

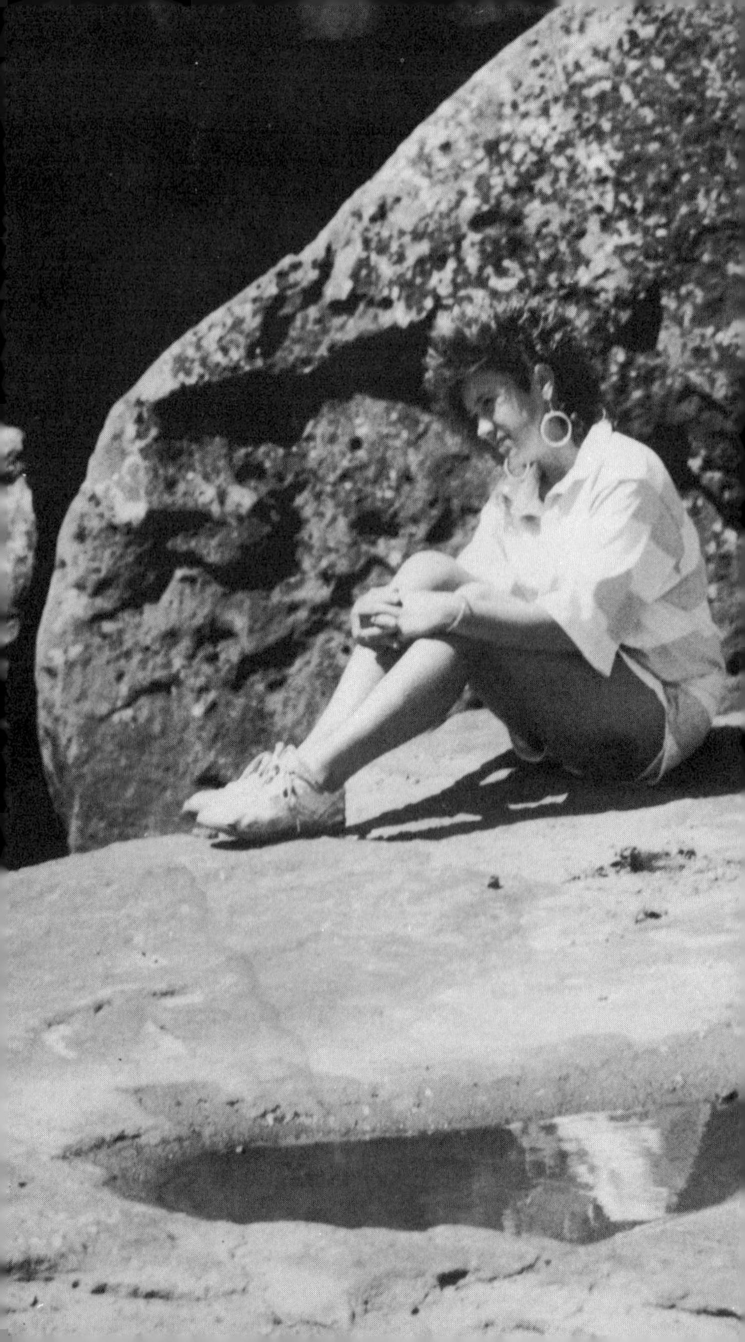

▶ **My rock**

O God,
I love to be in this spot,
lying back on my huge rock
staring up into your
light blue sky.
We are all alone
on top of the hill
looking across the pond.
I feel close to you, Lord,
here
in our private, secret
meeting place.
I come here to think together
with you,
about my day,
and important decisions.
Some days I imagine
you looking back at me
from behind wispy clouds
that part and hurry by.
I can't see beyond the blue,
I just know you're listening
to my thoughts.
Sometimes just being together
with you
and not saying a word
is the best part of the day.
I always feel special, Lord,
on my rock.

▶ Being sick is boring

Dear Lord,
I don't want to be
sick today!
I don't want to have
to stay in bed
and keep warm
and try and sleep.
I had plans for today!
We're having a movie
in history
and cheerleading practice
after school.
I don't want to miss science,
I get so behind and lost.
And I'd hoped to sit
with John at lunch!
Oh, c'mon, Lord,
I need to get well,
I don't have time to be sick!
Please!

▶ Not even once

Jesus,
I almost gave in.
It would have been so easy,
nothing to it, they said.
Just try it once to
see if you like it.
It scared me today, Lord.
I was so tempted
to try a little cocaine,
it was right there,
and my friend does it a lot.
I know drugs are wrong,
I've heard it all,
and what bothered me most was
it didn't matter.
I was curious.
How would I feel?
I wanted to know what really happens.
I thought it would be exciting
to take the risk.
Jesus, I never thought I was the type
who would give in under pressure.
I didn't,
and now I'm so thankful.
Keep me strong, Lord,
when I'm tempted and
want to listen to the crowd.
Help me say no so
I won't try it even once.

I don't get it!

Dear God,
if only my teacher knew
the real me!
The 'me' that can
make people laugh
and think I'm clever.
The part of me that
is creative and fun.
I want him to like me, Lord,
I look forward to his class
each day,
but he gets me all flustered
and nervous
when he calls on me.
He only sees that I couldn't
do my homework last night
and I have no answers
for these equations.
Lord, I just don't get it!
I'm not lazy,
just frustrated
and quiet because I need his help.
Give me the nerve to
stay after today
and ask him to
go over this stuff one more time!
I will do it, Lord,
I promise!

Forgive and forget

Lord Jesus,
I don't know how you do it.
They say that when
you forgive someone,
you forget that it ever happened.
It's like once I tell you
I'm sorry for what I did,
you won't mention it again.
Well, I'm having a hard time
doing that.
When a friend gets you in
trouble with your parents
and you're grounded,
it's hard to keep quiet.
Or when your little sister
breaks your tape player
or your hair dryer,
you remember!
And there's a certain satisfaction
you get in calling it to her attention
over and over again.
I'm trying to forgive and forget
because I know that's what
you want me to do.
I'm sure glad you don't
list all the things I've done wrong
and rub my rose in my sins.
Help me to do the same,
even with my little sister!

Looks aren't everything

Lord, you must just shake your head
and laugh at me!
So much time spent
fussing over a curl
or the way my makeup
covers a pimple on my chin.
I know it doesn't matter much
to you
how a person looks.
It doesn't matter if
my hair is too frizzy
and my chin is broken out.
You aren't impressed with
my fifty-dollar jeans
and my perfectly straight teeth.
Do you count the times
that I stare in a mirror
to see how I walk,
and if I'll catch the eyes
of the boys in the library?
Keep me from becoming a self-centered person,
I wouldn't want that.
I do care about others,
even those who aren't looking.
Make me more patient and kind
to them,
both girls and boys.
Make me into the person,
you want me to be.

Get well

Dear God,
nothing in the world
seems normal anymore.
There is always this
heavy sadness
pushing against my chest.
I only have one prayer,
one request,
that I repeat over and over.
My brother has cancer.
I can't believe it's true.
They found a lump in his lung
yesterday,
and doctors can't operate.
There are so many tests
and so many questions.
All I'm asking
is that you make my brother well.
I never wanted you to hear me more.
You've just got to listen!
I'm counting on you,
your healing power,
to help the doctors heal him.
He has to finish school
and play on the tennis team
this spring.
He's so disappointed and
serious now.
I hurt so much for him.
I know you can do it,

and you love him even more than I do.
Don't let him suffer.
Please lift the sadness from our hearts,
and fill us with hope
that you are already at work
making him well again.
Hurry, Lord, hurry.

Cold war

What makes it so hard to
make up, Jesus?
We had a fight,
and said some awful things,
and now we don't talk at all.
I avoid her in the halls
and imagine she's telling
terrible lies about me
to all her other friends.
Lord, I try to practice
what I'll say
when we finally get together.
At home
it seems so easy.
I'll say "I'm sorry"
and tell her I want to break this silent war
we've been having for a week.
But when I get to school
and see her ignore me on purpose,
I get angry again
and I walk in the other direction!
I do want to make peace with her;
we're both just being proud.
Jesus, give me the courage
to make the first move
and not back down
when I see her tomorrow!
I want the fighting to stop.
I want to be friends again.

My mean side

Dear Jesus,
there's a mean side of me
that creeps up now and then.
A side that likes to
tease and mock,
criticize and attack:
Mom and Dad,
neighbors,
classmates,
and even my best friends.
It's like a spiral,
I hurt others,
then I hate myself for
being so mean.
I don't understand
why I get so grouchy and
why I have to hurt
the ones who love me most.
Turn me around,
I want to change my ways.
Bring out that warm,
gentle side of me
that is patient and playful.
Give me eyes that see
a person's good points,
not just her faults.
Give me a heart full of love
with no room for bitterness.

Shower solo

Listen to that, Lord!
Can you hear that beautiful,
resonant soprano voice?
Such quality and clarity!
I love to sing in the shower,
water pouring down,
soap lathering,
and steam rising,
accompanied by my musical favorites.
A hit from the latest movie,
a little selection from
Sunday's choir anthem,
a rocking tune from the Top 40.
Nothing's too high or too low
for singing in the shower!
I feel great.
I'm not too bad.
What do you think?
Of course, I have *you* to thank
for my musical gift!
Now why can't I sing like this
when the choir director points
to me during rehearsal?
Nerves, I guess,
or is it acoustics?
Ahh, if she could hear me now,
I'd steal the show!

What to be?

Dear God,
I get so much advice,
I just want to plug my ears!
Dad wants me to go to college,
Mom wants me to program computers,
Grandpa thinks I show promise in languages,
and that's just great.
But I don't like any of those things!
I can't be what *they* say I should be
if it doesn't feel right.
Lord, you made us all different
as individuals,
and I have my own interests and goals.
At times, though, I feel guilty,
I want to make them happy because
they give me so much.
It won't disappoint them, will it,
if their daughter is a naval officer
or a telephone line worker?
I've thought of landscape design
or becoming a potter.
Who knows?
Please, help them relax
and stop pushing me into their mold.
I just won't fit!

▶ Getting a job

Oh, Lord,
what will I say?
Yes, I'll tell him,
I'm responsible and reliable,
honest and polite.
I want this job so bad,
and I'm so nervous!
Mom told me to "sell myself"
to the interviewer,
so he'll just *have* to hire me.
How embarrassing.
How can you be humble
and still brag?
Maybe I'm just not ready for this.
But I've wanted to earn some money
for so long.
Tell me, Lord, I can handle it.
Give me the right words
and the confident spirit I need.
Tell me you believe in me
and I'm perfect for the job!
I'm not a little kid anymore,
and I can handle it.

Bare branches

The tree outside my bedroom window
was so full and round
and colorful in October, Lord.
It looked cheerful and bright.
Now, when I stare outside,
I see a black and bare skeleton,
and the tree looks sad underneath.
After the leaves blow away,
I see things that were inside
the tree:
a flaky, old hornet's hive,
a bird's nest or two,
and a piece of tangled kite string.
Jesus, I think I'm like that old tree,
cheery and happy on the outside,
making people think I'm doing fine.
Yet you know the true me,
the emptiness I feel sometimes,
the sadness,
the old painful memories.
I cover them well,
so few people know what's inside of me.
Lord, I count on you
to get me through these lonely times.
There's nothing I can hide from you,
and I'm glad.
Give me the patience to wait
for time to pass,
and things will get better.
They always do.

Spring is coming
when my tree and I will
bloom and grow
from the inside out.

Why won't they come?

Dear Jesus,
I feel good about
being in church
and worshiping together
with all kinds of people
who want to be close to you.
I like to sing the songs
and to promise
I'll try harder to think
about other folks
and how I can help them.
I like the special feeling
I have when I take communion
and taste the bread and wine.
So I don't understand
what my parents have against church.
They won't come with me,
and it makes me feel bad.
I don't like to admit it
to the other kids,
so I make excuses for them.
I pray each week
that they'll change their minds
and sit beside me at worship.
Work on them,
and maybe sometime soon
I won't have to come alone.

Adopted

Dear God,
I love my mom and dad,
and I'd never want to hurt them.
I see the fear in their eyes
when I start asking questions.
I want to know, lately,
what my *real* parents are like.
I'm sorry, Lord,
I can't help wondering
if I look like my mother
or my father.
I can't help wondering
if they're young or old,
rich or poor,
eager to meet me,
or hoping I never find them.
Maybe it would be better
not to know more,
to leave things alone,
and spare all the pain.
What should I do?
It's just natural to be curious, right?
Comfort Mom and Dad,
assure them I'm not going anywhere
just because I want some answers.

▶ Walking on the beach

Whenever I come to the beach, Lord,
and hear the roaring of the waves as they
pound on the rocks
and the sand,
I feel so free
and fresh, it's amazing.
I stop and sit,
looking far out to sea,
and think faraway thoughts
about life and death.
Compared to the huge ocean,
my worries seem small.
I dig my toes in the warm sand
and smile at the beauty before me.
I feel at peace with myself,
my troubles roll out with the tide,
and I don't ever want to leave!
You're here
as I walk along the beach.
You are here.